Koṇārka

Chariot of the Sun-God

Koṇārka

Chariot of the Sun-God

Photographs: OKI Morihiro

Text: Bettina Bäumer
& M.A. Konishi

D.K. Printworld (P) Ltd.
New Delhi

Cataloging in Publication Data — DK
[Courtesy: D.K. Agencies (P) Ltd. <docinfo@dkagencies.com>]

Oki, Morihiro, 1929-
Koṇāka : chariot of the sun-god / photographs, Oki Morihiro ; text, Bettina Bäumer & M.A. Konishi.
vii, 138 p. 29 cm.
Includes bibliographical references (p.)
Contents: Chariot of the sun-god / Bettina Bäumer – Koṇārka : world heritage site, its geographical and historical position / M.A. Konishi.
ISBN 8124604363

1. Sun Temple (Konārak, India) — Pictorial works. 2. Architecture, Hindu — India — Konārak — Pictorial Works. 3. Sculpture, Hindu — India — Konārk — Pictorial works. 4. Sūrya (Hindu deity) — cult — India — Konārk. I. Bäumer, Bettina, 1940- II. Konishi, M.A. III. Title.

DDC 726.145 095 413 3 22

ISBN 10 Digit: 81-246-0436-3
ISBN 13 Digit: 978-81-246-0436-6

First published in India in 2007

Published and printed by:
D.K. Printworld (P) Ltd.
Regd. Office: 'Sri Kunj', F-52, Bali Nagar
Ramesh Nagar Metro Station
New Delhi-110 015
Phones: (011) 2545-3975; 2546-6019; *Fax*: (011) 2546-5926
E-mail: dkprintworld@vsnl.net
Website: www.dkprintworld.com

Contents

Acknowledgments

The idea for this book came when we were both Fellows at the Indian Institute of Advanced Study, Shimla, enjoying the peaceful atmosphere, green environment and an excellent library. A seminar organized by the Institute in Bhopal on the topic "Outlines of Indian Arts: Peaks of Creativity" (November 2004) under the chairmanship of Prof. G.C. Pande, gave us the inspiration, combined with the excellent photos of Mr. Oki Morihiro, who loves Koṇārka and has visited the site so many times. We are therefore grateful to the Indian Institute of Advanced Study for giving us the chance to work together and for using its facilities during our work on the book.

We also gratefully acknowledge the Alice Boner Foundation for reproducing the palm-leaf illustrations from Alice Boner's book, *New Light on the Sun Temple of Koṇārka*.

Finally, Mr. S.K. Mittal, our publisher, deserves all thanks and appreciation for his keen interest and untiring effort in bringing out this book in the best possible quality.

Bettina Bäumer & M.A. Konishi

Key to Transliteration

VOWELS

अ *a*	आ *ā*	इ *i*	ई *ī*	उ *u*	ऊ *ū*
(but)	(palm)	(it)	(beet)	(put)	(pool)
ऋ *ṛ*	ए *e*	ऐ *ai*	ओ *o*	औ *au*	
(rhythm)	(play)	(air)	(toe)	(loud)	

CONSONANTS

Guttural	क *ka*	ख* *kha*	ग *ga*	घ *gha*	ङ *ṅa*
	(skate)	(blockhead)	(gate)	(ghost)	(sing)
Palatal	च *ca*	छ* *cha*	ज *ja*	झ *jha*	ञ *ña*
	(chunk)	(catch him)	(john)	(hedgehog)	(bunch)
Cerebral	ट *ṭa*	ठ* *ṭha*	ड *ḍa*	ढ* *ḍha*	ण* *ṇa*
	(start)	(anthill)	(dart)	(godhead)	(under)
Dental	त *ta*	थ *tha*	द *da*	ध* *dha*	न *na*
	(path)	(thunder)	(that)	(breathe)	(numb)
Labial	प *pa*	फ* *pha*	ब *ba*	भ *bha*	म *ma*
	(spin)	(philosophy)	(bin)	(abhor)	(much)
Semi-vowels	य *ya*	र *ra*	ल *la*	व *va*	
	(young)	(drama)	(luck)	(vile)	
Sibilants	श *śa*	ष *ṣa*	स *sa*	ह *ha*	
	(shove)	(bushel)	(so)	(hum)	
Others	क्ष *kṣa*	त्र *tra*	ज्ञ *jña*	ळ* ḷ	ॠ* *ṝ*
	(*kṣatriya*)	(*triśūla*)	(*jñānī*)	(*play*)	

अं (ˆ) *ṁ anusvāra* (nasalisation of preceding vowel) like *saṁskṛti*
अः *visarga* = *ḥ* (aspiration of preceding vowel) like (*prātaḥ*)
ऽ *Avagraha* consonant #'consonant (like:- *ime 'vasthitā*)
Anusvāra at the end of a line is presented by m (म्) and not ṁ

* No exact English equivalents for these letters.

Introduction

Bettina Bäumer
& M.A. Konishi

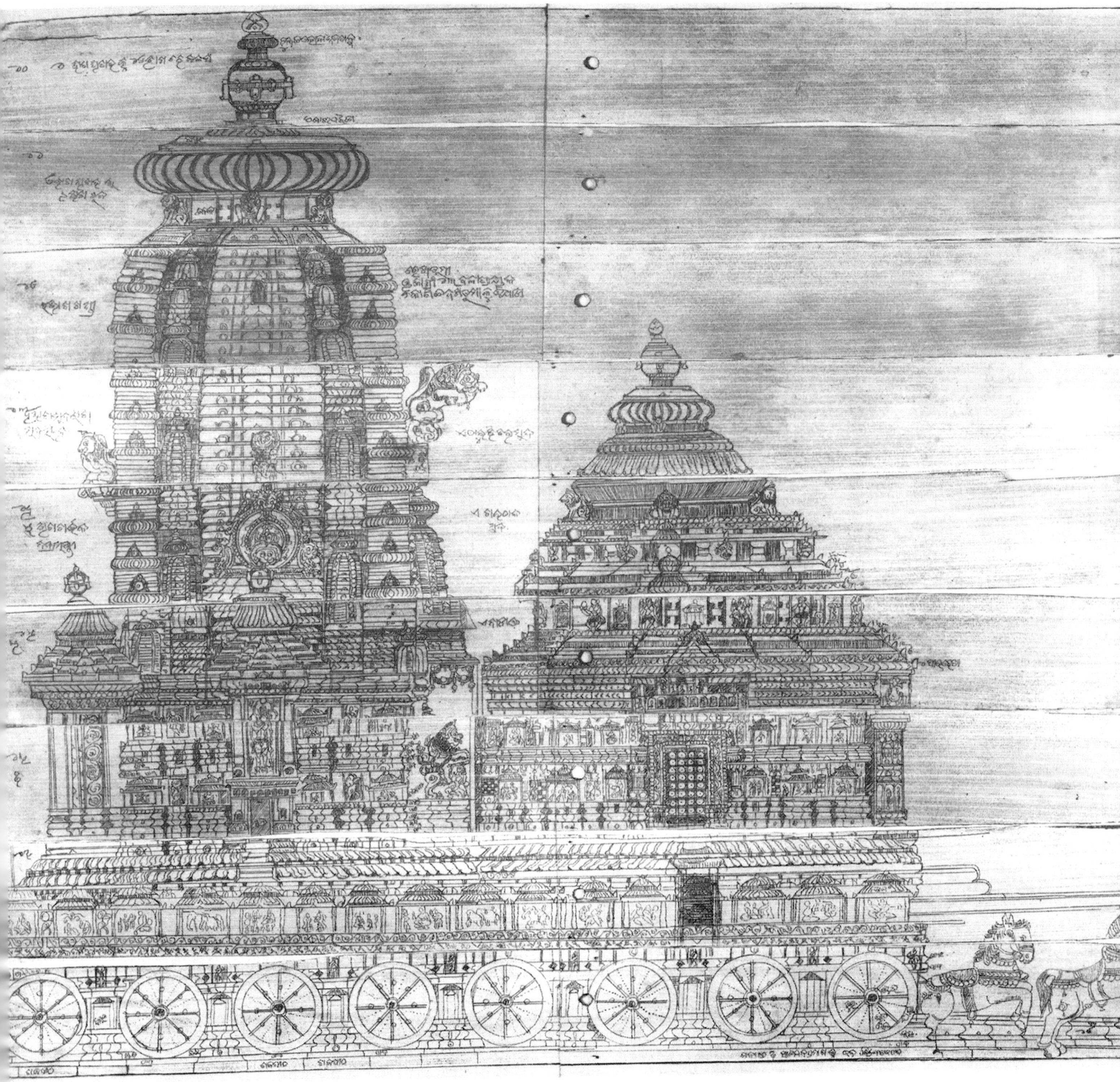

Palm leaf drawing of the complete temple
(from : A. Boner, *New Light on the Sun Temple of Koṇārka*)

Chariot of the Sun-God

Bettina Bäumer

Overview of the Sūrya Temple of Koṇārka

Orissa or the land of ancient Kaliṅga or Utkala, during and after the medieval period, has been celebrated for its richness in temples by pilgrims, explorers and archaeologists. Her most important sacred centres are dedicated to the four main deities: Koṇārka to Sūrya, Viraja or Jajpur to the goddess (Virajā, a form of Durgā), Ekāmra or Bhubaneswar with its Liṅgarāja temple to Śiva, and Jagannātha at Puri to the worship of Viṣṇu.[1] Among these the Sun-temple of Koṇārka had been the greatest, as can be seen even from the impressive surviving ruins. Situated at the east coast of Orissa, near the mouth of the (now dried up) Candrabhāgā river, the Koṇārka Sun-temple (popularly called Konarak, and earlier the "Black Pagoda") stands as a witness to the importance of the cult of Sūrya in ancient and medieval India, to the sacredness of the *arkakṣetra* or field of the Sun-God, as also to the greatness of its builder, Rājā Narasiṁha I who ruled during 1238-1264 AD, to his chief architect (*sthāpaka*) and the artists (*śilpī*) he engaged for this stupendous task. *Koṇārka* is understood to mean the [eastern] corner (*koṇa*) sacred to the Sun-God (*arka*), its other variant names being *Koṇāditya* (with the same meaning), *Padma-kṣetra* and *Bhāskaratīrtha* are also used for the site. The temple, even in its present fragmented state of ruins, is outstanding not only in size but also in its original conception and artistic uniqueness. It has been wrongly identified with the overlay of erotic sculptures (similar to the case of the Khajurāho temples) whose interpretation is still a matter of debate.

The grand vision underlying this temple is the chariot of the Sun-God, drawn by seven horses and equipped with twenty-four (twelve pairs) of stupendously carved wheels, which have rightly become the cultural symbol of Orissa. It is the image of the Vedic Sūrya transmuted into stone, combining the heaviness of a great architecture with the movement of a chariot. We shall explore this symbolism later.

The aim of this introduction is not to go into historical and archaeological details (for which see the literature appended in the Bibliography), but essentially to uncover the symbolism of the architecture and sculpture of the main temple and its two subsidiary shrines, the Mahāgāyatrī Temple and the Naṭa Mandira or Dance Hall at the eastern front side, in relation to the conception of Sūrya.

It is a frequent misunderstanding to hold that architecture and sculpture adhering to the rules and canons of Śāstra (texts on *śilpa* and *vāstu*) leads to a limitation in creative expression. Orissa has a rich literature of Śilpaśāstra[2] (see Bibliography), and yet the creativity of the *sthāpaka*s, *sthapati*s and *śilpī*s (architects and artists) has not been impeded. On the contrary, it has given them a framework within which they could operate to unfold their genius. Koṇārka is the clearest example for this relationship between precision and imagination, adherence to canons and innovation. It is also a luminous example for the integration of architecture and sculpture, so typical of the Hindu temple. In the words of A.K. Coomaraswamy, "it would be hard to find anywhere in the world a more perfect example of the adoption of sculpture to architecture."[3]

"The most ambitious undertaking during the Gaṅga period, and one of the most stupendous projects ever attempted in India, was the construction of the Sūrya Deul at Konark during the reign of Narasiṁha I" (Donaldson 2003:17). It was this king who was not only a successful warrior, but also a visionary, a generous and learned ruler, a great devotee and an expert in art (he is called *silpajña*)[4] who conceived this temple. It was a revolutionary undertaking for two reasons: one, the Sūrya (or Saura) cult was no more a dominant religion in thirteenth century Orissa, and two, the very size and conception of this stupendous monument. But he could undertake this task only with the help of the master architect (*sūtradhāra*), Sadāśiva Samantarāya Mahāpātra, and his group of expert architects and sculptors, whose names are mentioned in the text *Baya Chakaḍā* or chronicle of the construction and book of accounts, translated by Alice Boner in her important work, *New Light on the Sun Temple of Koṇārka* (Boner 1972). Here we get to know the names of the artists, the most outstanding being: Gadādhara Mahāpātra (chief executive architect), Gaṅga Mahāpātra (head of the *śilpīs*), Nārāyaṇa Mahāpātra (master sculptor) and Viśvanātha Mahāpātra (sculptor specialized in royal scenes). We know from Boner's study that architecture and sculptural works were undertaken by groups of architects and sculptors under the supervision of master artists who were specialists in deciding and directing the themes to be carved. Thus we see the masterpieces that could have been done by the masters, while the more simple and decorative carvings by the less experienced hands.

According to tradition, the building activity took twelve years — and the number twelve is symbolic for the entire temple, for Sūrya and the legends associated with it. Thus even the number of *śilpīs* engaged in the building is given as 1200. The date of completion or rather consecration of the cult image of Sūrya and the first day of *pūjā* (ritual of worship) performed by the King is recorded in the *Madalā Pañji* chronicle as Sunday, *Māgha Śukla Saptamī* or the seventh day of the bright half of the month of Māgha, in 1258 AD.

Ever since its rediscovery in the late eighteenth century, after the collapse of the *vimāna* (spire or *śikhara*) in the seventeenth century (ca. 1628 acc. to *Madalā Pañji*), the temple has given rise to a number of questions and speculations as well as legends which are even today more popular than the historical facts, but we need not go into these in the present context. We may refer only to one question which concerns the reason of the destruction of the *vimāna*. There were speculations that the temple was never completed, or that it was destroyed when Orissa was invaded by Kalapahāḍa in 1568. Both conceptions have been proved erroneous. The temple which had been consecrated in 1258, remained under worship at least until

1610. It was probably in 1628 that, owing to a structural imbalance, the colossal *gaja-siṁha* (lion on the back of an elephant) projecting from the spire on the eastern façade fell down, and with its weight pulled down the wall and damaged the image of worship. It is said that this dislocation was the result of king Narasiṁha pressing the architects to speed up the work so that the temple could be completed on the auspicious day when the bright seventh *tithi* of the month of Māgha fell on a Sunday. With the collapse of a part of the spire the temple started disintegrating and worship of the shrine ceased.

We are not going any further into the later history of rediscovery, plundering and repair of the monument, and for these, one could see Donaldson (2003: 26-34 et al.).

Sun-worship in India and the Sanctity of Arkakṣetra

The Sun has been revered as the great cosmic symbol of the Divine power of Light and Life in almost all civilizations, and Sūrya has been worshipped in India since the time of the *Ṛgveda*, and praised in a number of hymns, and in many of his aspects and names, such as Savitṛ, Pūṣan, Mitra, Āditya. Uṣas or the Dawn is his female counterpart, one of the few feminine deities of the Veda, and described in highly poetical hymns. The imagery of Sūrya riding on a chariot drawn by seven horses through the sky, from sunrise to sunset, is a Vedic conception which has inspired the artists at Koṇārka.

His shining beams now introduce
the God who knows all living things,
that all may see the Sun. (1)
You shine upon the host of gods
and likewise on the race of men, that all
may see the heavenly Light. (5)
You steer your path across the sky,
O Sun, across the realms of space,
measuring the days by means of your shining,
observing all that comes to birth. (7)
Seven bay mares drawing your chariot

conduct you, O far-seeing God,
Sūrya of the flaming hair. (8)[5]

— *Ṛgveda* 1.35.2-4

Sūrya or Savitṛ is the life-giving and inspiring force, it is he who oversees all things on earth and who maintains cosmic and moral order (*ṛta* or *dharma*). He is also the great fertilizing energy, and therefore the hymn celebrating the marriage of his daughter Sūryā with Soma is even today used in the Hindu marriage ritual (*Ṛgveda* 10.85). This connection with fertility is certainly one of the background conceptions of the much disputed erotic imagery of Koṇārka.

As Savitṛ the Sun-God is invoked in the *Gāyatrī-mantra* for inspiration and enlightenment:

oṁ tat savitur vareṇyam
bhargo devasya dhīmahi,
dhiyo yo naḥ procodayāt

— *Ṛgveda* III.62.10

"We meditate upon the glorious splendour
of the Vivifier Divine,
may he himself illumine our minds."[6]

The symbolism of light in its physical and spiritual dimensions is central to this *mantra* which is recited at the three junctures or *sandhyā* of the day by orthodox Hindus: sunrise, noon and sunset. No wonder that Sandhyā is one of the Śaktis of Sūrya, and that the subsidiary shrine to the great Sun-temple is dedicated to Sūrya's Śakti, Mahāgāyatrī. She is the *mantra* personified.

But the temple with its entire complex symbolism is not only a visual concretization of the Vedic Sūrya with his many aspects and associations, but of the Tāntric development of the Sūrya cult or Saura Tantra. This tradition has not continued and we also have very few surviving texts, but it has been influential in Orissa in medieval times.

Sūrya is the giver of life (the root *su-* meaning to impel, to vivify, to enliven, to beget), but he is also the source of time and hence identified with Time, as expressed in the *Maitrī Upaniṣad*:

> "It has been said that food is the origin of this whole world, that the origin of food is time, and, again, that the origin of time is the sun. The form of time is the year, which consists of twelve months and is composed of moments and other measurements of time . . . . It has been said: As many divisions of time as there are, in all of these moves yonder sun. . .
>
> This embodied time is the royal ocean of creatures. In it stands he who is called Savitṛ, the impeller, from whom the moon, stars, planets, the year, and everything else is begotten. And from them comes the whole world, as well as whatever is good or evil in this world. Therefore *Brahman* is the self of the sun. Indeed one should revere the sun under the name of time. Some, in fact, say: "*Brahman* is the Sun."
>
> — *Maitrī Upaniṣad* 6.14-16[7]

Thus Sūrya stands for Light, Life, and Time — and all three are manifested in the great symbolism of the Koṇārka temple.

Apart from Vedic and Tāntric sources, the Purāṇas also play an important role in both, the sanctity of the site and the legends associated with the temple. *Brahma Purāṇa* describes the glory of Koṇāditya in the holy land of Utkala or Oḍradeśa (Ch. 26. 1-29): "The Sun-God known as Koṇāditya is the lord of that land. Those who visit lord Bhāskara there are liberated from sins . . . The shrine of lord Sun is famous in the whole world. The region all round to the extent of a Yojana yields worldly pleasure and salvation. The thousand-rayed lord Sun is directly present there. He is well-known as Koṇāditya. He is the bestower of worldly pleasures and liberation." (26. 17-18). This *kṣetra* fulfils all desires, especially it bestows health to the sick, knowledge to the learned and sons for those desirous of progeny (26. 43). It is clear that all these aspects are present in the great temple which, like the Sun-God himself, can bestow worldly pleasures, health, fertility, intellectual and spiritual insight, depending on the devotee who approaches it.

A number of Purāṇas as well as the *Bṛhat-Saṁhitā* testify to the sanctity of the *Arkakṣetra*, also called *Padmakṣetra*, *Mitravana* etc., already in the sixth-seventh century, and the site must have been sacred even before that. The collective memory of the people is much stronger than historical records, and the festival, described in great detail in the *Brahma Purāṇa*, obviously goes back to a much earlier time, and it is celebrated even today: *Māgha Śukla Saptamī* or the seventh day of the bright half of Māgha is the day when thousands of pilgrims not only of the surrounding villages, but also from great distances, flock to Koṇārka to celebrate the birth of the Sun-God from the sea. For them it does not matter that the temple is in ruins, as Sūrya is for them a living divinity and the sacredness of temple and sea-shore comes alive when they stand in expectation of the sun-rise and take bath in the sea or in the pond left over by the Candrabhāgā River.

The legend of Sāmba, the beautiful son of Kṛṣṇa, recorded in the *Sāmba Purāṇa* and others, is associated with the origin of Sun-temples. Sāmba was cursed by his father for having tried to seduce his wives and was smitten by leprosy. It was only by meditating on and worshipping the Sun-God for twelve years that he could be cured of the disease, and he became a fervent devotee of Sūrya. Originally this legend was connected with the Mūlasthāna or Sāmbapura in Punjab (present-day Multan in Pakistan), but it was later transferred to Koṇārka which is equally said to have been the place where Sāmba was cured from leprosy by the blessing of Sūrya. The same name of the river Candrabhāgā occurs in Multan and at Koṇārka (also in other places). According to this legend, Sāmba found an image of Sūrya in the Candrabhāgā river. "The image spoke to him and asked him to build a temple for its worship. When the temple was finished and Sāmba did not know whom he should call for officiating in it, the Sun-God himself asked him to fetch from Śakadvīpa (Iran) some Magas [priests] who were Sun worshippers and were also versed in medicine. He thereupon brought eighteen families of Magas from Iran for the worship in this temple" (Boner, 1972: xxiv).[8]

The *Sāmba Purāṇa*, the oldest portion of which goes back to the early sixth century, reflects the history of the Saura religion and its Iranian influence. When the Kuṣāṇas conquered Northern India in the first century AD and ruled for a century and a half, with their capital at Mathura, the Iranian and Scythian influences were merged with the Vedic Sūrya. Maga priests were brought from Iran to officiate in the Sun temples, and the iconography of the Sūrya image was influenced by the dress of a Kuṣāṇa ruler or Scythian warrior, with high boots and a close-fitting tunic. This dress is described in the *Bṛhat Saṁhitā* as *dhyāna* of Sūrya, and the high boots have been retained in all later images, following the prescription that his legs should be covered.[9]

The story of Sāmba also creates an interesting connection between Kashmir and Orissa, or rather, the Sun cult and Kashmir Śaivism. The eighth century Sūrya temple at Mārtaṇḍ in Kashmir shows the importance of Sun worship in Kashmir. With the decline of a separate Saura tradition, and with the rise of Trika Śaivism from the eighth-ninth centuries, Sūrya was absorbed in Śiva, and the conception of Mārtaṇḍa Bhairava is a result of this merging. In Koṇārka, too, an image of Śiva-Sūrya was found,[10] and the dancing free-standing figures of Bhairava on the roof of the *mukhaśālā* have been identified as Mārtaṇḍa Bhairava by C. Sivaramamurti (1961). But more than this, the philosophy and mysticism of the Sun has been poetically described in an early Kashmiri text, the *Sāmbapañcāśikā*, equally ascribed to Sāmba who got healed by composing and reciting it.[11] This hymn complements the missing theology of the Koṇārka temple, and makes it clear in terms of Kashmir Śaivism or Trika. It is now certain that there were links between Kashmir and Utkala, which were most probably established by wandering Śaiva ascetics and priests, as testified by ritual manuals.[12] This text which propounds *kuṇḍalinī yoga*, starts with a verse describing the symbolism of the seven horses of Sūrya, implying the seven notes of the musical scale, the seven colours, the seven *ṛṣis*, the seven metres, besides the seven days of the week etc. The importance of sound (*nāda*) in connection with Sūrya is an important aspect (verse 2), and Sūrya is identified with Consciousness and called *cidarka*, as well as *paramāditya*. An interpretation of the Koṇārka temple in mystical-philosophical terms may be undertaken with the help of this text.

Temple Architecture and Symbolism

In the background described so far, it is clear that the Koṇārka temple is not only housing the Sun-God (Sūrya Deul), but in its total conception and architectural-sculptural execution,[13] a metaphor of the Indo-Iranian divinity in all its aspects:

cosmic, human and divine, or, in one word, "cosmotheandric."[14] The Sun being "the light of the whole world," his temple also reflects all the dimensions of reality, from the sublime spiritual aspects of light down to the cosmic and human life and to the animal world, but all this in the manner of an ordered whole. This structure has the form of a heavenly chariot with twelve pairs of richly carved wheels, symbolizing the twelve months or the twenty-four half-months (*pakṣa*) of the year, consecrated to the twelve constellations, and drawn by seven horses, the seven days of the week, with all the other implications of the number seven. It is the great chariot of Time in which the whole world moves and has its life. The high platform (3.9m), called *cakrapīṭha* in the Śilpa texts (see *Śilparatnakośa*, vv. 58-63), heightens the impression of the chariot, and binds together the two main elements of the temple: the *mukhaśālā* or hall, which alone remains now, and the *vimāna* or spire which is reduced to a fragment. The wheels (2.9m in diameter) have eight major spokes, with a medallion carved with images in each, and eight thin rods — again the number sixteen is significant (see Plates 21-30). The wheels rest on a beam with an elephant frieze (Plate 31). The elephants (more than 1700 in number) are represented in various activities, and in a lively way, including a scene of catching them in the forest. According to Boner, this frieze is also a tribute to the contribution of elephants in the construction of the temple.

The design of the temple is called *Mahāpraśasta Pañcaratha Prāsāda*, and it presents an enlargement of the *Mahākailāsa* type, as exemplified in the Liṅgarāja temple at Bhubaneswar. *Pañcaratha* means with five vertical projections on the spire or *śikhara*, and *mahāpraśasta* could be translated as the "highly praised." "The temple is built with exactly the same structural elements and with the same proportional relations between its various parts. Only its *mūlasūtra*, its fundamental unit of measurement, is one and a half times that of the *Mahākailāsa* temple, and thus the entire temple would attain to one-and-a-half times the height of the latter" (Boner 1972: xxxviii). Even the still standing *mukhaśālā* (without the crowning *kalaśa*) is impressive by its height (39m), but the *vimāna* or spire is estimated to have been 68.5m tall. Due to its size, the pyramidal roof of the *mukhaśālā* in *pīḍha* design has been divided into three horizontal tiers (unlike two tiers in other temples), in the intervening spaces decorated with the great figures of female musicians and Bhairavas, carved in the round. "The play of light and shade between the projections and recesses of roof and walls are so precisely and delicately balanced that they create spontaneous elation in every beholder" (Boner 1972: xxxvii). The high understructure of the *mukhaśālā* is characterized by three great stairways, the eastern one leading to the finely carved portal, and the northern and southern leading to *gavākṣa* openings.[15] All these elements add to the "nobility and monumentality" (Boner, ibid.) of the temple. We shall come to the sculptures separately, although they are an integral part of the architecture.

The *vimāna* was flanked by three lateral or *niśā* shrines, housing the great images of three aspects of the Sun-God (these images are now framed by reconstructions). Inside the *garbhagṛha* or sanctum the richly carved platform housing the main *pūjā* image has survived (see Plates 51-52), the image having been removed before 1628 to the Jagannātha temple in Puri.

The architecture of both, *mukhaśālā* and *vimāna*, follows the canons of Orissan Śilpaśāstra, and yet there is a free play with the elements. The base, called *pañcakarma* in the texts, and popularly *pābhāga* ('foot-part'), consists of five mouldings which represent the five cosmic elements: earth, water, fire, wind and ether.[16] Though this is common to all Orissan temples, it emphasizes the cosmic aspect of the Sun-temple. An important aspect of the symbolism of the temple is the Sūrya-*yantra* (mystical diagram) underlying the ground plan of *mukhaśālā* and *vimāna* (Boner 1972:210-212).

Without going into the architectural details of the main temple, we shall now see the other two important monuments in the compound connected with the Sūrya temple: the Mahāgāyatrī (or Māyādevī) Temple to the south-west of the main temple, and the Naṭa Mandira or Dance Hall at its eastern front.

1. The **Mahāgāyatrī Temple** (also called **Māyādevī**) is dedicated to the Śaktis of Sūrya, according to the *Trikāla Mahāmāyā Arcanā Vidhi*, translated by A. Boner (Boner 1972:39-44): Mahāgāyatrī, Sāvitrī and Sarasvatī. Stylistically the temple has been assigned an earlier date, eleventh and twelfth centuries (Donaldson 1993: 9, 15), and Donaldson identifies it with an earlier Sūrya temple on the basis of the iconography, since the *pārśva devatā*s are Sūrya images, of which

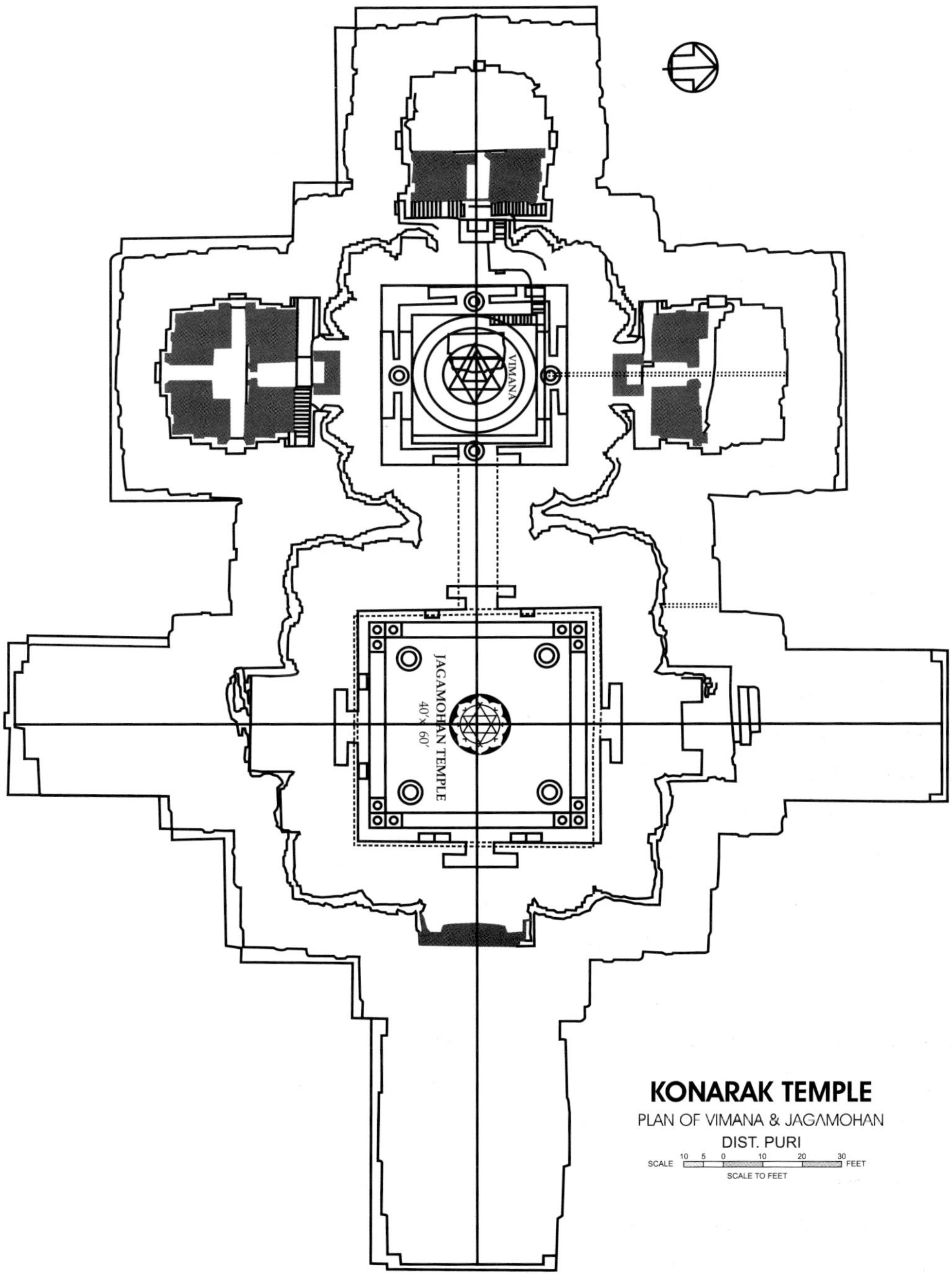

Groundplan according to Archaeological Survey of India, also represents *yantra*s underlying *garbha* and *mukhaśālā*. (from : A. Boner, *New Light on the Sun Temple of Koṇārka*)

Haridaśva (or Bhāskara) in the north and Mitra in the south are still intact, in spite of the delapidated condition of the temple. But after the construction of the great temple this must have been converted into a temple for the Śakti (or Śaktis), as described in the ritual text. The *Trikāla Mahāmāyā Arcanā Vidhi* assigns the three *Devīs* to the three juncture times of the day, when Sūrya is to be worshipped along with his Śaktis: Mahāgāyatrī before sunrise, Sāvitrī at noon, and Sarasvatī at the evening twilight. The text states that the worship of Sūrya without his *tejaḥ-śakti* (luminous power) would be fruitless, and along with chanting the *mantra* and *dhyāna* or meditation verse it also gives the three *yantra*s of the Śaktis which are underlying the three sections of the temple. The rituals testify to an integration of Vedic and Tāntric elements.

2. The **Naṭa Mandira or Dance Hall** stands as an independent building to the east, facing the entrance (see Plates 5-20). It is laid out on a square *yantra* of the nine planets, consisting of nine compartments (15.8m square). Based on a high platform (3.6m) are sixteen broad pillar-walls, four of which are massive central ones. Broad stairways lead up on all four sides. The roof is now missing, but it must have been a sloping pyramidal structure whose inner ceiling has survived, a beautifully carved lotus medallion (see Plate 8; now preserved in the Koṇārka Museum). The platform is *pañcaratha* (with five projecting parts) and divided into two wall-sections above the *pañcakarma* base. "Their surface is treated in delicate undulating rhythms by the stepped wall-pilasters and smaller vertical elements" (Boner 1972: xxxlx). The entire building is pulsating with life, just as the dance and music that used to be performed there, because of the lively figures of dancers and musicians, in various poses of dance, with various instruments, including humorous scenes and the dance-master or *ācārya*, as well as mythical figures of rampant *virāla*s in all the niches and on pilasters. No portion of the wall is left plain, so that the heaviness of the stone is as if overcome in a playful manner and becomes transparent.

Sculptural Creativity

The richness and creative spirit of the Koṇārka sculptures has been summarized most aptly by Alice Boner who has truly thrown "new light" on this master work. In her words:

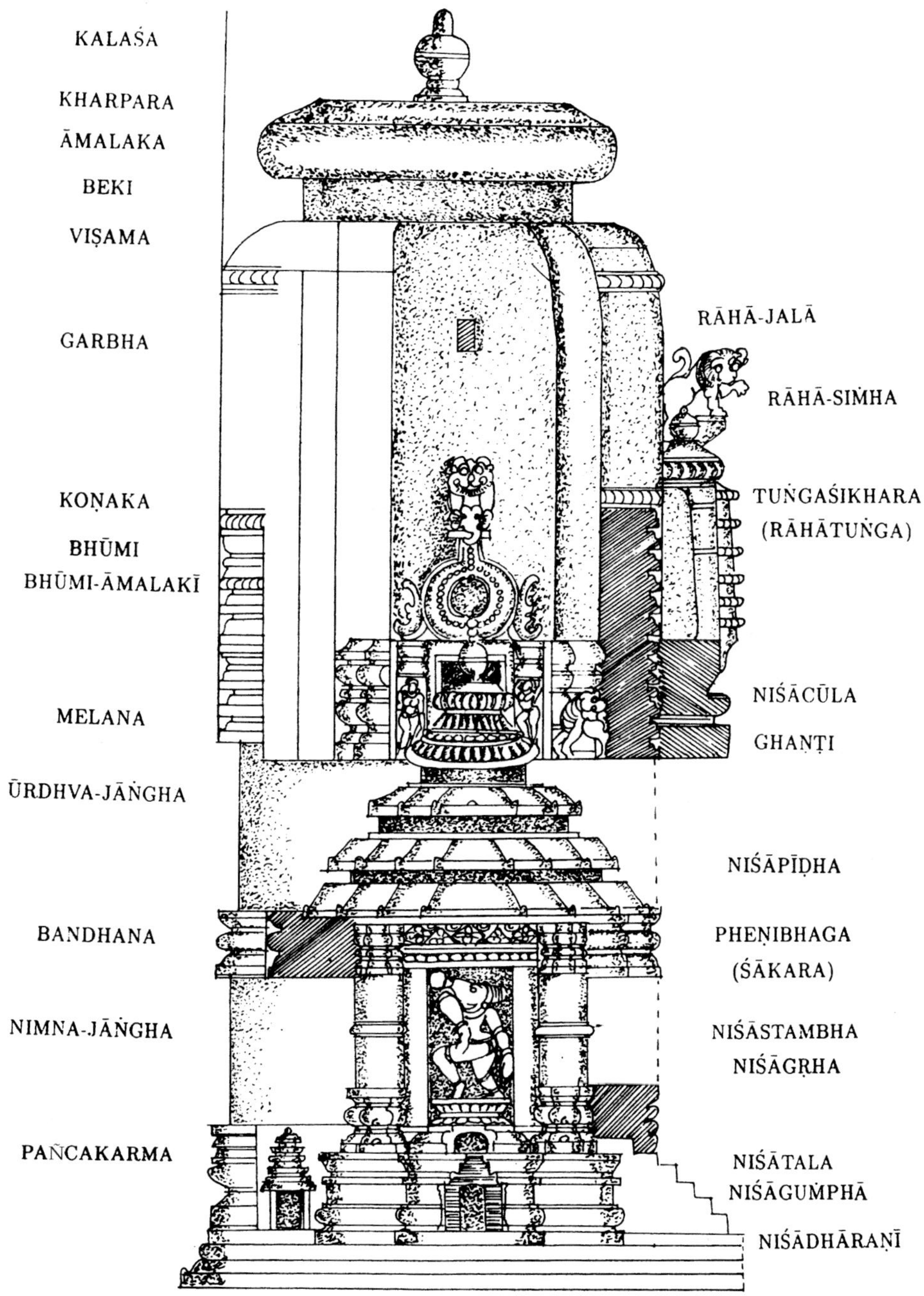

Vimāna or *rekha śikhara* with *niśā* side-temple

> The temple bears the imprint of a powerful spiritual current that animated its builders, from the man who conceived the plan to the artisans who carried it out. Although it is the last of the great Orissan temples, a fresh vision and a new vigor are here infused into traditional forms. The repertory of motifs prescribed by rules of iconography not only appears in unusual formulations, but is enriched by many hitherto unknown subjects. An unprecedented outflow of imagery in its exuberant imagination and its immense love and passion for life leaves no sphere of existence untouched. It expresses all shades of feeling, from adoration of the transmundane and divine to admiration of royal glamour and splendour, from exaltation of living beauty to the passions and emotions of ordinary worldly life. Even the queer, the odd and the grotesque, treated with a superior sense of humour, are not out of bounds. In the acceptance of life in all its aspects the imagery has so-to-say adopted the view of Sūrya himself to whom nothing is hidden, who looks upon everything in perfect equanimity, who smiles upon life and recognizes the inevitable necessity of opposites in the interplay of light and darkness, of Sattva and Tamas.
>
> — Boner 1972: XXXIII

One could not express the overall vision and display of images more beautifully.

In terms of Indian aesthetics or *rasaśāstra* this means that all the nine *rasa*s and *bhāva*s as described in the *Nāṭyaśāstra* are applicable to the sculpture displayed on the Sun-temple,[17] most prominent among the eight or nine *rasa*s being *śṛṅgāra rasa* or love in all its aspects, from the delicate to the gross, uninhibited sexual poses of the *mithuna* couples. *Hāsya* or humour is evoked by grotesque ascetics and playful monkeys; *vīra* or heroism and even *raudra* or anger are evident in the royal and battle scenes, including the *gajasiṁha / gajakrānta siṁha* motif of the lion pouncing upon an elephant, the war horses and elephants; *adbhuta*, wonder or surprise in many of the composite *virāla* figures, some of which also evoke *bībhatsā*, revulsion, or *bhayānaka*, the fearful sentiment. *Karuṇa rasa* or sorrow and pathos is not easily found, except in some minor scenes.[18] But the final *rasa*, *śānta*, is visible in the serene, peaceful, divine images of Sūrya. The overall dominant emotion brought about by the total imagery of the temple is, as Abhinavagupta says, joy or bliss: *ānanda*. The wide variety of sculptures can

also be described on the basis of their size, their placement, or the themes represented. In fact, everything is connected and no sculptural or decorative element can be isolated from its context in the total scheme.

We may only highlight some of the masterpieces and dominant motifs. As mentioned earlier, the main *pūjā* image of Mahābhāskara is no longer *in situ*, and it is supposed to have been placed inside the Jagannātha temple in Puri. K.S. Behera has established its identity (Behera 1996, Vol. II: 213-214), which also corresponds to the drawing of the image in the palm leaf manuscript on architecture (Boner 1972: Plate 76) showing a seated serene form of Sūrya holding two lotuses in his hands[19] (see p. 19). The extant *mūrti*s are the three aspects of Sūrya in the lateral niches (*pārśva-devatā*): Mitra in the South, Pūṣan in the West and Haridaśva in the North, riding on a well-caparisoned horse (see Plates 45-50). These tall (3.4m) hieratic images, placed inside a *toraṇa* and surrounded by subsidiary figures, radiate the glory of the Sun-God by their serene faces (*śānta*) and upright bodies. We need not go into a detailed description of the entire panels, but to add a word by Boner: "The figures of the Sun-God are far superior to the best sculpture produced in Bhuvaneśvara two centuries earlier. . ." (Boner 1972: xxxvi). Other *pārśva-devatā*s include the *dikpāla*s (guardians of the directions) and their consorts placed in the lower and upper niches of both *mukhaśālā* and *vimāna*.[20]

The monumental images on the roof of the *mukhaśālā* deserve special attention, for they are unique in their style: the female musicians or Apsaras playing different instruments (drums, cymbals, *kahalā* or a kind of *śahanāī*), and the four-headed and six-armed Bhairava, dancing on a boat, protecting the temple. Above every door-frame there was a *navagraha* panel showing the nine planets, and the one from the main (eastern) entrance is now preserved and worshipped in a shed outside the temple compound (see Plates 39-41). It consists of a row of the nine planets, which are important on every temple but more so in the context of Sūrya, the Lord of planets. Other masterpieces of sacred images are preserved in the British Museum: a Naṭarāja, a Mahiṣāsuramardinī, a five-headed Śakti-Gaṇapati and a Sūrya. They all display the unique features of the Koṇārka style.

But what has given Koṇārka its fame is the so-called erotic sculpture or the abundance of *mithuna-mūrtis* (loving couples) in all sizes and poses, although we must not forget that "the actual number of explicit sexual scenes at Koṇārka . . . is actually small in contrast to the profusion of other images" (Donaldson 1993:60). It has been noted that the erotic theme is not specifically related to the cult of Sūrya, since it is found profusely on other Orissan temples as well. It has been said to belong more generally to the Tāntric trends of the time, although there is hardly any depiction of Tāntric sexual rituals as such. Many of the theories trying to explain the role of erotic images on the temple have been proved wrong or at least one-sided.[21] Apart from the very general conception that the love-theme is common to literature, art and sculpture (Behera 1996, II: 239), we may endorse here only two interpretations, based on the Śilpaśāstras. One is the architectural symbolism of the relationship between *mukhaśālā* (hall for the devotees) and *vimāna* (sanctum) or *garbha* (literally, womb) which is described as one between bride and bridegroom. Even today the juncture (*sandhisthāna*) between the two is called *gaiṇṭhala* in Oriya, i.e. the knot tying bride and bridegroom together at marriage; but not all *mithuna* sculptures are placed at the juncture recesses.

The *Śilpa-Prakāśa*, which is dated earlier than the Koṇārka temple (see Bibliography) places the love images, called *kāmabandha* or the couples "tied in love," in the wider and deeper symbolic context of *śilpavidyā*:

> "Love is the root of the universe. From love all beings are born. The primal elements and all beings are again reabsorbed through love. (499)
>
> Without Śiva and Śakti creation would be nothing but mere imagination. Without the action of *Kāma* there would be no birth or death. (500)
>
> Śiva himself is visibly manifested as the *Mahāliṅga*, and Śakti in the form of the *Bhaga* (womb). By their union the whole universe comes into being. This is called the action of love (*kāma-kriyā*). (501)
>
> The science of *kāmakalā* (*kāmakalāvidyā*) is an extensive subject in the *Āgamas*. A place without love-images is known as a place to be shunned. (502)
>
> In the tradition of the *Kulācāra* it is always a base, forsaken place, resembling a dark abyss, which is shunned like the den of Death. (503)

Palm-leaf drawing of main Sūrya image (now in the Jagannāth temple, Puri)
(from : A. Boner, *New Light on the Sun Temple of Koṇārka*)

> Without offering *pūjā* to the *kāmakalā-yantra*, the Śakti *pūjā* and the *sādhanā* (spiritual practice) become as useless as the bath of an elephant."(504)
>
> — *Śilpa-Prakāśa* II.499-504

Underlying some panels of *mithuna* is the *kāmakalā yantra* which is known only to the initiated *Kaula* or proper worshipper of Śakti, but which assures the protection of the temple and its worshippers and bestows all perfections or *siddhi*s (*Śilpa-Prakāśa* II.536).

> "This *yantra* is utterly secret, it should not be shown to everyone. For this reason a love-scene (*mithuna-mūrti*) has to be carved on the lines of the *yantra*.
>
> In the *Kaulācāra* tradition it should be made on the lovely *jāṅgha* [vertical wall] in the upper part of the wall. The *Kāmabandha* [or *Mithuna* figure] is placed there to give delight to the people." (II.538-539)

The relationship between *yantra* (symbolic diagram) and *mūrti* (actual images) is that between the esoteric and the exoteric meaning of these sculptures, meant for different kinds of people and their respective level of approach.

Mention should be made also of the superb *nāga* and *virāla* figures found in the recesses of the lower *jāṅgha* (wall-part) and on the *pīṭha* (plinth). Their symbolism is also important as they link the cosmogonic level with the cosmic conception of the temple. Both motifs are apotropaic in function. The *virāla*s being composite animals or animal-human figures constitute transitional moments, both vertically and horizontally, protecting the spaces in between. The well-preserved door-frame of the main entrance portal is a masterwork, consisting of seven bands of decorative motifs, including an intertwined snake couple or *nāga bandha*.

Thus the sculpture of Koṇārka ranges from the monumental to the miniature; from the sacred to the secular including the royal scenes; from the playful (the dancing *devadāsī*s and musicians at Naṭa Mandira) to the solemn figures of gods and saints; from the cosmic (the planets) to the Divine; embracing the multiplicity of life in all its dimensions.

Tradition and Creativity

The Koṇārka temple complex embodies both, the tradition of Orissan temple architecture as well as its culmination. The *Nāgara* or the Northern style *śikhara* of the no longer extant *vimāna* or the sanctuary follows the *rekha* style taking the shape of a spire, and the *mukhaśālā* follows the *pīḍha* or pyramidal pattern, both according to the Śilpaśāstras. And yet, these architectural forms are not only magnified in size, but also glorious in imaginative architectural and sculptural originality: the high platform with the wheels and horses, the contrast between the monumentality of the main temple and the elegant Naṭa Mandira, and the many creative polarities between sculptural elements as described above. These polarities encompass above all the divine, the cosmic and the human dimensions of the universe that the temple represents, Sūrya being the great symbol inspiring all these realms of existence: *prāṇabhṛt Sūrya ātmā*, "Sūrya is the inmost reality of all, the carrier of life" (*Sāmbapañcāśikā* 24). No doubt, one of the fundamental polarities of human life which is sought to be integrated in the grand vision of this temple is the male-female polarity. It can only be integrated in the light of the Sun of consciousness (*cidarka, citsūrya*; cp. *Sāmbapañcāśikā*).

As a post-face a remark about the possible restoration of the temple may not be out of place: On the basis of her study of the temple and the manuscripts related to the architecture and construction history, Alice Boner had made a proposal to UNESCO in 1977 for restoring the temple by replacing the architectural fragments and scattered sculptures in their original place. Apart from sculptures kept in Museums and transferred to other temples like Jagannātha in Puri, the entire area around the temple complex is strewn with stones from the temple, which could be collected and replaced in their original context, replacing the ugly plain walls. It would also be possible to empty the *mukhaśālā* of the filled-in rubble and restore the interior. If a much bigger monument such as Borobudur could be dismantled and reconstructed for the sake of restoration, this should also be possible in the case of one of the greatest sacred monuments of India, Koṇārka.

Notes

1. This is also confirmed by a panel on the *vimāna* of the Koṇārka temple, in which its builder, Rājā Narasiṁha I pays obeisance to the three other deities: Durgā Mahiṣāsuramardinī, Jagannātha and a Śivaliṅga. See Plate 53, and Donaldson 2003: 25, Photo 4.
2. We are using the architectural terminology as described in these texts instead of the popular terms, viz. Oriya *Deul* (Sanskrit *devālaya*) is called *vimāna* or *śikhara* as in the *Śāstra*, and *jagamohana* is called *mukhaśālā* as in Sanskrit texts.
3. A.K. Coomaraswamy; quoted by Donaldson 2003: 2.
4. Cp. *Ekāvalī* by Vidyādhara.
5. *Ṛgveda* I.50, transl. R. Panikkar, *The Vedic Experience*, 1977: 322-323, Cp. also *Ṛgveda* IV.13.
6. Ibid., 38.
7. Transl. Panikkar, *The Vedic Experience*, 1977: 223-224.
8. Cp. R.C. Hazra, *Studies in the Upapurāṇas*, vol. I, Calcutta Sanskrit College Research; H. von Stietencron, *Indische Sonnenpriester,* Wiesbaden: Otto Harrassowitz, 1966.
9. *Matsya Purāṇa*, ch. 261, etc. See Plates 45, 48, 50; and also the descriptions given by Rao 1914-15, Banerjea 1956 et al.
10. Now placed in the Koṇārka Museum.
11. *Sāmbapañcāśikā*, ed. and transl. into Hindi by Svāmī Īśvara Svarūpaji, Srinagar 1976. Cp. a partial English translation: Bettina Bäumer, "Sūrya in a Śaiva Perspective. The Sāmbapañcāśikā. A Mystical Hymn of Kashmir and its commentary by Kṣemarāja" in: *Sahṛdaya, Studies in Indian and South-East Asian Art in Honour of Dr R. Nagaswamy*, Chennai: Tamil Arts Academy, 2006, pp. 1-28.
12. Cp. the *Paippalādavaṣādiṣaṭkarmakāṇḍapaddhati*, ed. by Umakant Panda, Balasore, 2003.
13. Another example in Orissa is the Rājārāṇī temple in Bhubaneswar, which is an embodiment of the goddess Rājarājeśvarī. Cp. *Śilparatnakośa* (Mahapatra, 1994.)
14. A term used mostly by R. Panikkar; cp. *The Vedic Experience*, 1977.

15. These two stairways were originally flanked by monumental war-horses and elephants facing outward, which are now placed on separate platforms in the compound (facing towards the temple).

16. Cp. *Śilparatnakośa*, vv. 70-102.

17. For an application of *rasa* to the temple, cp. B. Bäumer, "*Rasa* and Temple" (unpublished paper, presented at a Seminar on *Rasa* in B.H.U.) Cp. *Viṣṇudharmottara Purāṇa*, *Citrasūtra*.

18. Such as the moving leave-taking scene. Boner 1972: Plate 16 d; and Plate 67 of this volume.

19. Similar to the well-preserved sculpture in the British Museum. Behera 1996, II: Plate 85.

20. Only five have survived, see Donaldson 1993:54.

21. Cp. Behera 1996, vol. II: 230-240, where he surveys the different interpretations of the erotic theme (strangely omitting a reference to Alice Boner's book).

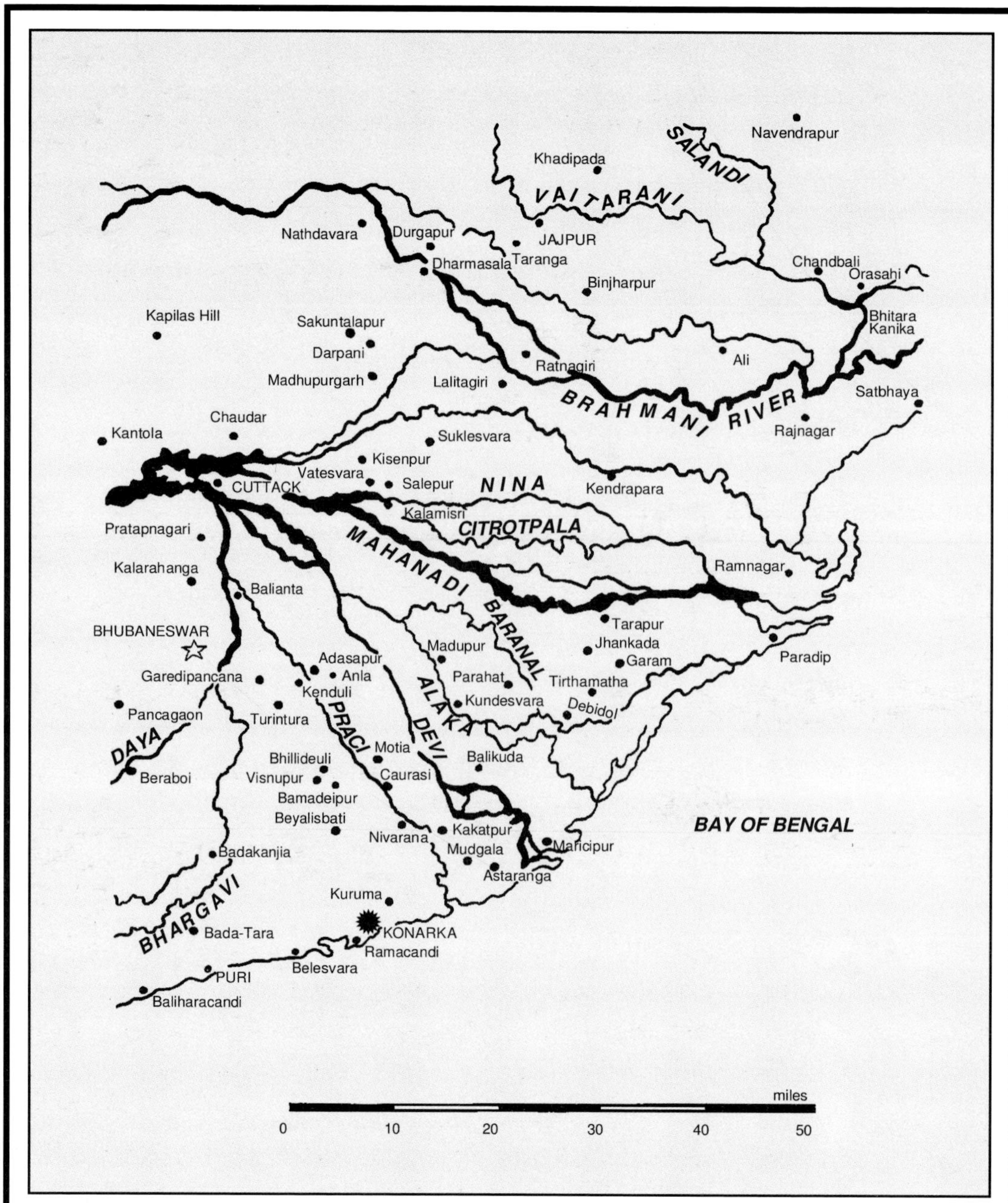

Map of the Mahanadi Delta

Koṇārka — World Heritage Site

Its Geographical and Historical Position

M.A. Konishi

Orissa – Land and Culture

Orissa where the Temple of Sūrya stands is unique in respect of geography and history of the Indian Sub-continent. Linguistically, Oriya or the major language spoken there belongs to the Indo-European Family as do the Eastern Hindi in Bihar and Bengali in West Bengal. The general northern characteristics are noticeable in Orissa's cultural aspects, including sculpture and architecture, arts and crafts and other folk heritage. However, we should note that geography and history of Orissa is quite complex. The hilly and mountainous side in the west adjacent to Chattisgarh has a predominance of the tribal culture, and the *ādivāsī* (indigenous) cultural influence is obvious. We may see it even in the Jagannātha cult that has been Sanskritised as a form of Vaiṣṇavism, and the numerous *grāmadevatā*s or village gods and goddesses that are locally worshipped.

The eastern half of the land is a vast plain fed by mighty rivers including the Mahānadī that they have developed fertile deltas on which rich royal cultures and powerful dynasties flourished since ancient times. They had trades and cultural contacts through land routes connecting Orissa with more "authentic" Gangetic cultures, introducing the "Aryan" aspects of religious beliefs and rituals of the Northern Plains, or even those from Kashmir as has been discussed by Dr. Bäumer. However, the "Gangetic" aspects have been brought more directly from the adjacent Bengal, which has itself been a complex mixture of various cultures, a cultural drift or a depot with *ādivāsī* cultures both from the west through Chotanagpur Plateau and northeastern regions of Assam and further northeast, as well as the Northern or "Aryan" standards along with the flow of Gaṅgā through its fertile plains, and the Southern or "Dravidian" to such of cultures through Orissa as the corridor open to the vast coastal plains spreading towards Andhra-deśa and further south. The delta and the fertile coastal plains could have served as good sea-trade ports open to the Bay of Bengal, and the Temple of Koṇārka is erected in such a geo-cultural position. We have evidences of extensive archaeological and ethnological studies about the locale, but that is not the main subject for our present discussion.

Historically, Kaliṅga flourished in Orissa during the early centuries of history. It was a mighty kingdom particularly in the third century BC as we know from the famous edict of the Mauryan emperor, Aśoka, whose army killed several *lakhs* of the people of Kaliṅga. He extended his rule not only all over the North but also the entire Sub-continent, and established his principle to rule by *dharma*. Śiśupalgaṛh on the east of Bhuvaneśvara or present Bhubaneswar has flourished from third century BC to fourth century AD and has served as the capital of this and later dynasties. Even right after the collapse of the Mauryan empire, Kaliṅga flourished particularly under a prominent king Khāravela who rose in Kaliṅga as early as first or second century BC, and annexed vast parts of the South as well as the Gangetic regions. He was a devout Jain, and Orissa has served as an important centre of Jainism along with Buddhism for a long time. In spite of the repeated rules by the Gupta and Pāla from the North and the Coḷa and Vijayanagar from the South, Orissa under the name of Utkala gave birth to original cultures under less powerful but characteristic local dynasties during eighth-thirteenth centuries. Especially during twelfth-thirteenth centuries, architectural masterpieces came up in Orissan style in hundreds particularly in and around Bhubaneswar, and at the sacred places like Puri and Koṇārka.

Koṇārka, a World Heritage

The architecture of Orissa represents a typical North Indian Nāgara style, in some way similar to the temples of Khajurāho in Bundelkhand, although the

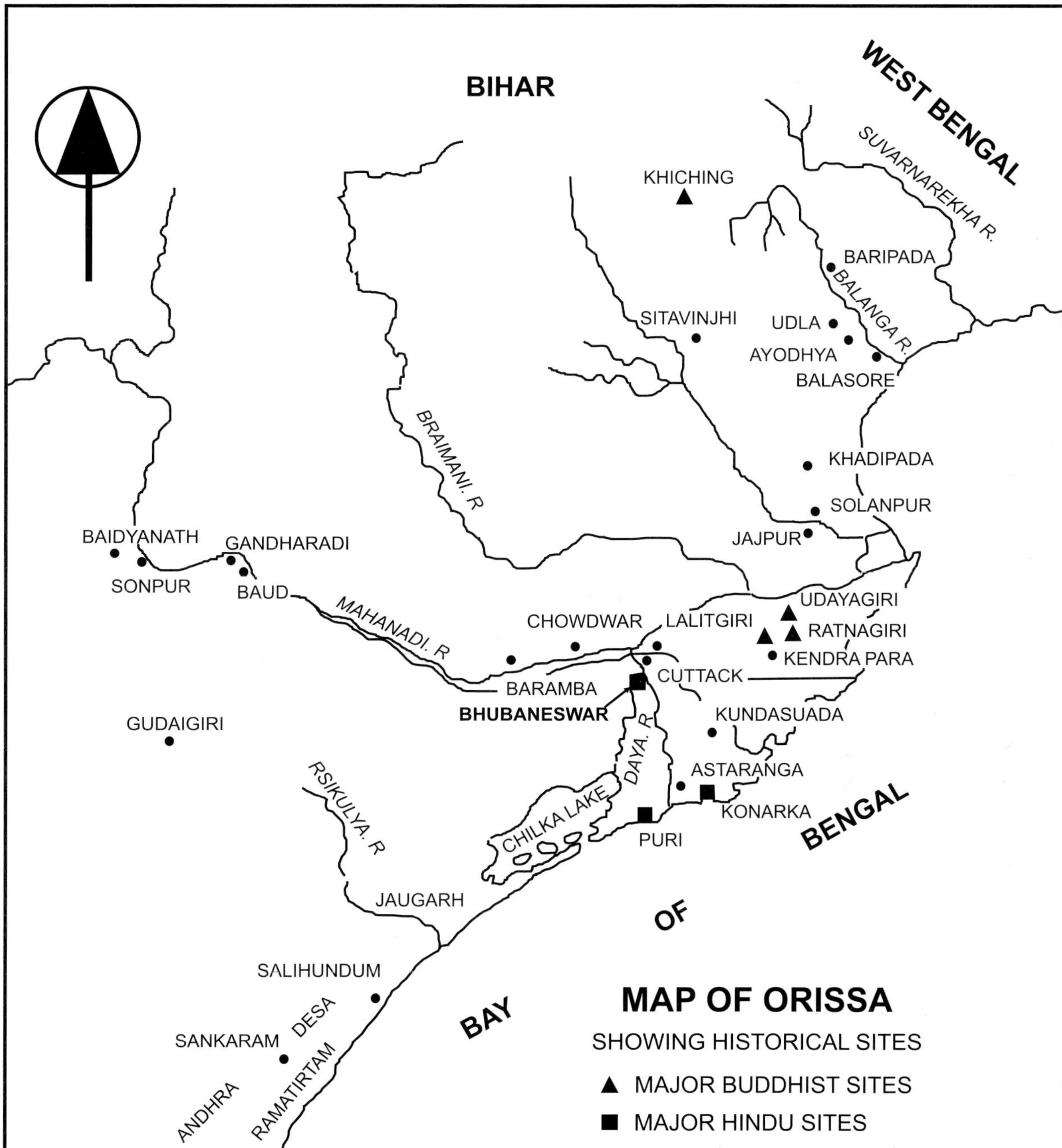

After Behra,1996 (revised)

frontal shrine (Mukhaśālā, *jagamohana* or *pīḍha-deul*) is not crowned by sharp pinnacles like Khajurāho temples. There are rows of superimposed flat roofs (called *pīḍha*) to form a squat pyramidal form as a whole, a Southern or Dravidian feature. The Orissan Temples can be broadly divided into three periods of their creation. The first period (750–900) is represented by Paraśurāmeśvara and Vaitāl Deul Temples in Bhubaneswar. They show South Indian influence of the Cāḷukya and Pallava architecture but with more powerful and massive sculptures. The second period (900–1100) is represented by Mukteśvara Temple, small but charming in harmony of beautiful architecture and sculptures, and Rājārānī Temple known by its exquisite sculptures. The best examples of the last period (1100–1250) are the grand Liṅgarāja Temple at Bhubaneswar and Jagannāth Temple at Puri, which are quintessential of Orissan architecture, with their magnificent *śikhara* of the main shrine (*vimāna* or *deul*) and the artistic carvings. These architectural features finally culminate in the Sun Temple of Koṇārka at the end of the period, built by Narasiṁha or Narasiṁhadeva I of the Later Gaṅga Dynasty.

The Sun Temple of Koṇārka is unique in having two important buildings in its compound [See Site plan]. One is the Mahāgāyatrī Temple remaining at the south-western corner of the precinct, showing the origin and development of Sūrya worship and the architectural styles. Another unique and important structure besides the main shrine is Naṭa Mandira to the east, placed in front of the Mukhaśālā. It is a beautiful structure on which devotional dance and music used to be performed. The whole structure is decorated with intricate and fine sculptures of celestial musicians and dancers.

Naṭa Mandira has not always been an essential component in a temple compound of the Nāgara style of temple architecture, though we see in Kerala *Koottambaram* or special performance stage set within the wooden temple compound. The carved figures of dancer-musicians as we see here at Naṭa Mandira as well as Mukhaśālā of Koṇārka have been later adopted as the model for dance postures of Odissi dance on reviving the classical dance form in early 20th century, as was the case of sculptures of Bṛhadīśvara and other temples belonging to the Coḷa Period (eleventh century) showing all the 108 *karaṇa*s or

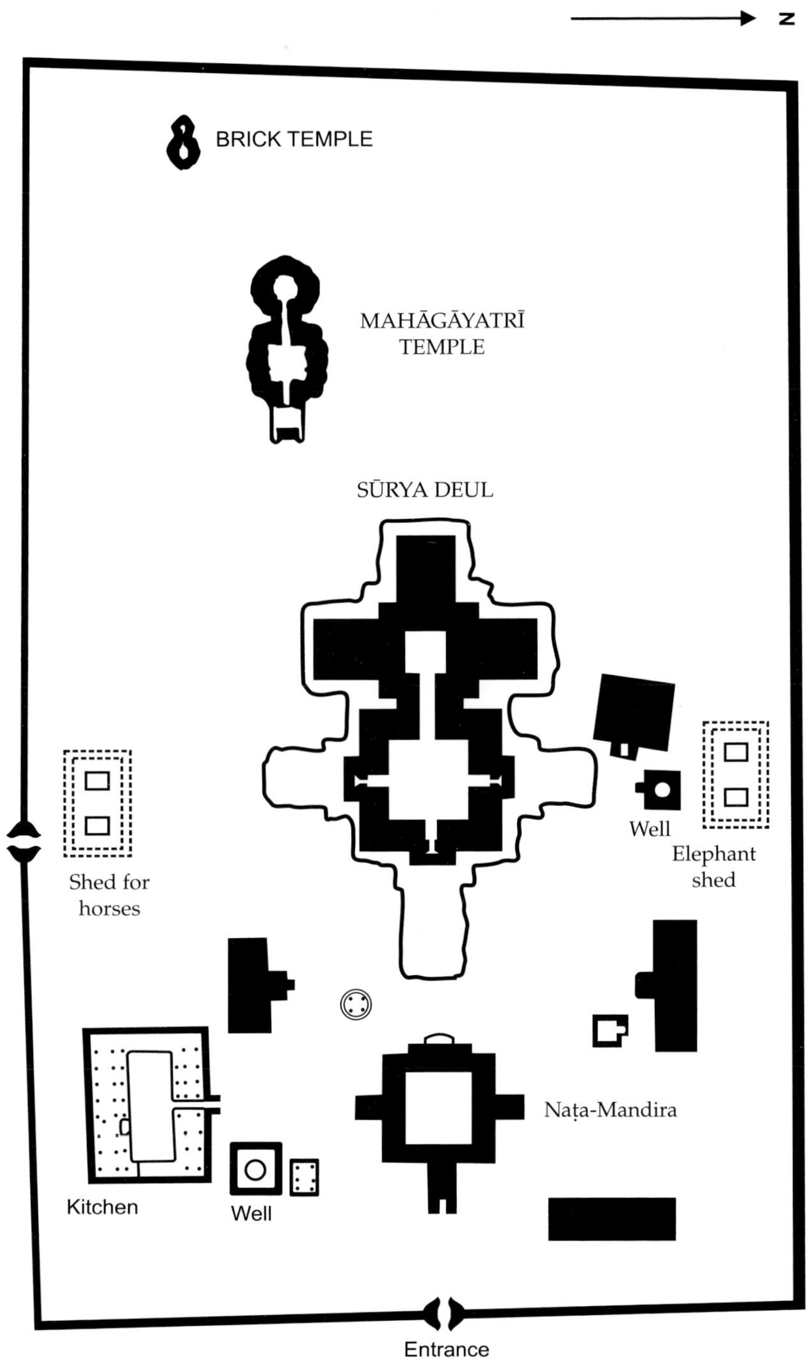

Koṇārka Site Plan (from: Donaldson 2003)

dance postures later to be adopted in more modern forms of Bhāratanāṭyam. By these sculptures we can well see the close connection between the temples and rituals with dance and music throughout the time (see Plate 103).

Koṇārka has been registered by UNESCO as a World Heritage since 1984, now among the 25 World Heritage Sites in India (of them 20 are cultural sites). Future development plans have been proposed since then with a scope of "cultural tourism of the Golden Triangle" in Orissa, comprising of Koṇārka, Puri and Bhubaneswar. Sarangi's master plans with maps and planning proposals for the development around Koṇārka monuments and the surrounding villages are noteworthy (Sarangi, 1990). Serious planning for cultural tourism for casual visitors, too, is needed for all such World Heritage Sites, besides the more technological restoration and conservation not only of the monuments but also of the environmental ecology, for the sake and development of the local people, especially in such an economically retarded state like Orissa. Heritage is not a matter to be pushed in the Past, but an integral component to be developed among the people, especially by and for the local people living in the Present.

(From: Brown 1959)

Description of the Plates

1. The Sūrya Temple complex at Koṇārka, an aerial view taken from the south-east. Note that the main temple buildings are set on the east-west axis, facing the east from where the Sun rises over the Bay of Bengal. To the right corner is seen the frontal shrine Naṭa Mandira serving as the Festive Hall, and *mukhaśālā* (or *jagamohana*) of the Sūrya Deul is behind it in the centre of the complex. The main sanctuary behind it formerly with its high *śikhara* has fallen down leaving the lower portions, with only the *siṁhāsana* or the platform for the main Deity in the interior. The broken Mahāgāyatrī or Māyādevī Temple, the earliest of the complex, can be seen at the extreme left corner.

2. Roof of the Hall or *mukhaśālā,* following the style of *pīḍha-deul* with pyramidal roof The picture shows the upper parts with bell-shaped and circular *āmalaka* on the top (the *kalaśa* or "vase of fullness" formerly crowning the top is now missing). The total height at present is about 39 m from the ground. In the recess between the series of flat *pīḍha*s or tiers of the roof are set fully carved sculptures of lions and human figures (see also Pl. 56).

3. The southern side and rear view of the *mukhaśālā* Hall. The whole structure is conceived to represent the Chariot of the Sun moving towards the east, drawn by seven horses at the front (seen at the extreme right of the photo) and 24 huge wheels originally set on the platform-wall of the temple.

4. Galloping horses in front of the Hall pulling the chariot-temple. Now only a few horses are remaining in the front, all in movement towards the sky. The lively style carved in the round is noteworthy among the sculptures of Koṇārka, as most of the sculptures are otherwise carved in bas-relief.

5. Naṭa Mandira, Festive or Dance Hall seen from the south-east. Four flights of steps lead one to the high platform, where devotional dance rituals used to be performed as part of the worship of the Sun-God.

6. Lions pouncing over elephants in front of Naṭa Mandira. A pair of fierce lions of gigantic size guard the eastern main entrance of Naṭa Mandira. Triumph over the mighty elephants shows the even mightier power of lions, symbolizing possibly the founder-king, Narasiṁhadeva (not in the original site).

7. Frontal view of Naṭa Mandira seen from the east. The roof over the upper pillars is missing but should have been pyramidal to culminate to the height of a *śikhara* behind, that is also missing now.

8. The original ceiling of Naṭa Mandira, carved in dark chlorite stone, now in the Koṇārka Site Museum. In the centre is seen the figure of Sūrya riding on the heavenly chariot drawn by seven horses, and 8 and 16 lotus petals surround it, representing as a whole the wheel of the chariot of the Sun-God travelling through the universe.

9. Naṭa Mandira seen from the back or the west. The structure faces the east or the Bay of Bengal to receive the first ray of the rising sun. Note that the western stairs are equipped with three moonstones on the top.

10. Rows of musicians and dancers on the base wall of the Naṭa Mandira. Detailed and intricate carvings have given much inspiration to the contemporary and later musicians and dancers.

11. Bracket above the upper platform. Water spout as a female *praṇāla* figure whose voluptuous bust and extended open thighs might symbolise the concept of fertility (*Lajjā Gaurī*?).

12. Śiva in an inset of the basement of Naṭa Mandira. A miniature but charming piece of art, showing the Deity on his *vāhana*, Nandī.

13. Kṛṣṇa as a flute player in an elegant *tribhaṅga* or three-bent posture, with a small figure of a lady attendant.

14. Musicians. To the left is a pot-bellied *vīṇā* player, and to the right is a lady playing on a *ghaṭam* or pot-drum, placed over her thighs and beaten by both hands.

15. Musicians. To the left is an aged man playing *ghaṭam*, and to the right is a jovial lady playing *mṛdaṅgam* or *khol*, a barrel-shaped horizontal drum.

16. A player of *kahalā* (a kind of wind instrument) in *tribhaṅga* posture.

17-18. Musician-dancers, playing *kahalā*, *mṛdaṅga* and *vīṇā*. The elegant poses have been adopted in dance postures especially on reviving the Odissi style of dance in recent time.

19-20. Musicians, showing the male ascetic players of *vīṇā* and *ghaṭam* (19), and the lady playing cymbals to keep time or *tāla* (20).

21. Southern side of *mukhaśālā*. Gigantic wheels of the chariot temple are impressive with intricately carved 8 major spokes and 8 subsidiary spokes.

22. Southern wall of *mukhaśālā*. Note the position of the wheel just below the icon of Mitra, or the Morning aspect of Sūrya.

23. First frontal wheel on the Southern wall near the entrance flight of stairs of *mukhaśālā*, which is badly damaged now.

24. Middle of the southern wall. The lion placed on the left of the wall is not in original position.

25-28. Medallions on the spoke depicting various aspects of life including a hunting scene (26), and some of them are erotic in nature (27-28). Note that lying figures on bed have not been carved on the generally vertical pillars or recesses of the Temple.

29-30. Medallions on the frame of the wheel. They are all nicely arranged within a decorative creeper, spotted with intricate designs of birds, animals, plants and geometric designs (called *gumphana* in the Śilpaśāstras).

31-38. Lowermost friezes below the wheel. The gigantic wheels do not rest directly on the ground but are placed on a thin band of decorative friezes all around, carved with rows of horse and elephant battalions (31), march with the general in a palanquin (32, 35), battle and hunting scenes (33, 34, 36-38), etc. Musicians also accompany the army to cheer up (36), and a wooden fort is being constructed at the front (38).

39-41. *Navagraha* or the Nine Planets (seven planets with *Rāhu* and *Ketu*), originally placed above the central door jamb of the eastern portal. Most important objects for the pilgrims and worshippers, but now dismantled and kept apart and worshipped in a shed outside the north-east corner of the compound.

42. *Navagraha* on the door jamb photographically restored to original position. A composite reconstruction on the plate.

43. Friezes of the central door jamb. Minute decorations on the entrance doorway, but the interior is now totally filled by rubbles to avert the danger of collapse.

44. Detail of the left frieze of door jamb. Above the rows of deities at the bottom rise vertical bands of decorative friezes with creepers and plants, *nāga* or entwined serpents, miniature *caitya* windows, etc.

45. Sūrya as Mitra on the wall of the southern side-Temple. Prominent as it is carved in round using hard dark-green chlorite, the image looks majestic with attendants, and the chariot below his feet is drawn by seven horses.

46. Detail of Mitra's head. Serene with spirituality, yet sensual with his big nose and thick lower lip. A real masterpiece of the time.

47. Seven horses under the Deity to pull the chariot. Narasiṁha Varman and his *purohita* or royal priest kneel at the feet of the God in a worshipful pose.

48. Sūrya as Pūṣan on the wall of the western side-Temple. Another majestic figure of the Deity looking west to witness the sunset and ensuring the repeated sunrise, or the universal cycle.

49. Detail of Pūṣan. Though carved in stone, the warmth of flesh can be felt under the fine lace of accessories hanging from the waist and the thin drapes of the *dhotī*.

50. Sūrya as Haridaśva on the wall of the northern Side-Temple, riding on a horse. The balance of the figures of Sūrya and the horse is superb — here the horse is more than his *vāhana* (vehicle), it is a part of him.

51. Detail of *siṁhāsana* (royal throne) of the ruined sanctuary on which the main Deity or *pūjā* image was placed. A fine carving of elephants in frieze is seen at the base.

52. Full view of the *siṁhāsana* for the main Deity, now exposed, leaving only the vacant platform (the image is now placed inside the Jagannātha Temple in Puri).

53. A panel on the wall, showing Durgā, Jagannātha and a Śivaliṅga (upper left), and to the right king Narasiṁha receiving the garland of command from his *guru*.

54. Apsaras or heavenly musician playing *kahalā* in a pensive mood. Carved in the round and resting on the middle *cāla* recess of the roof of *mukhaśālā*.

55. A lady drummer (Apsaras) on the middle recess of the roof. One of the most famous masterpieces among the Koṇārka sculptures.

56. Upper portions of *mukhaśālā* showing tiered *pīḍha*, *ghaṇṭīcāla* (bell-shaped roof) and *āmalaka*. Note the well planned positions of lions and musicians.

57. Heavenly musicians in the recess of the middle row of *cāla*. Here a lady plays small cymbals to keep time, *tāla* of music and dance.

58. Musicians and Mārtaṇḍa-Bhairava on the tier, composite figure of Sūrya and Bhairava, dancing to create the universe to the rhythm of *ḍamaru* (a small hand-drum) held by one of his left hands, with a *cakra* in his front right hand. See also Plate 63.

59-61. Group of celestial musicians on the tier, playing *kahalā* (wind instrument) and cymbals in devotion.

62. Apsaras playing cymbals. Feminine beauty is well expressed in her facial expression and high bust.

63. A side-view of Mārtaṇḍa-Bhairava, composite figure of Sūrya and Bhairava, showing three heads and four hands. See Plate 58.

64. Sculptural panels and pilasters on the Wall. Upper panels, from left to right: *mithuna* or an amorous couple, foreign delegates (66), and the *sūtradhāra* couple (65). *Nāga* and *Nāginī* are shown below in a row.

65. A happy and peaceful couple: *Sūtradhāra* or the architect and his wife, who must have contributed to the construction of the Temple.

66. Foreign delegates dressed in long skirts bringing tributes to the king riding on an elephant, including a giraffe. Though it is uncertain how Orissa had contacts with Africa, overseas trade must have been active on the shore of the Bay of Bengal during this time.

67. Pathetic departing scene of an old lady leaving her family. She blesses her son while the daughter-in-law bows down to her feet and the grand child clings to her.

68. *Alasākanyā* (graceful maiden) as *Ḍālamālikā*, holding the branch of a tree. *Yakṣiṇī* or *Śālabhañjikā* has been a popular motif in Indian sculpture since early centuries AD.

69. *Kanyā* or maiden putting on earrings. Later adopted as a popular posture of Odissi dance, including other postures of toiletry (70-73).

70. Joy of life with full feminine energy.

71. *Ḍālamālikā*, or *kanyā* holding a branch of a tree.

72. *Nūpurapādikā*, or *kanyā* removing the anklets.

73. *Darpaṇā*, or *kanyā* looking into the mirror, also a popular toiletry scene.

74. A naked woman standing over a flame. There may be a magical or symbolic meaning in it, but the significance is uncertain.

75. Warriors with horse. A powerful group-sculpture which reminds of a modern sculptural work.

76. Galloping horse pulling the chariot-temple. Animal sculptures in large size are a typical feature of Koṇārka art.

77. Mighty elephant overpowering an enemy, who lies lifeless but still holding the shield. Elephants played a prominent role in the battlefield, and also in the construction of the Temple.

78. Lion pouncing over an elephant. Stylised lions have protruding eyes to add to their fierce look.

79. *Virāla* or composite animal, rampant over a demon or evil-doer, called *Dharmavirāla*. *Virāla* is an apotropaic motif in Koṇārka and in other Orissan Temples, where they appear repeatedly in various combinations on pillars and in recesses.

80. Possibly a giraffe, or a winged antelope, a rare motif.

81. *Nāga* and *Nāginī* or serpent couples entwined in an amorous posture, symbolizing fertility and protection.

82. Amorous couples or *mithuna*, alternately set with *Nāga-Nāginī* figures.

83. Amorous *Nāga-Nāginī* couple and a musician. Charming combination of *Nāga* and human figures.

84-85. Amorous *Nāga-Nāginī* with gracefully extended arms.

86-90. Amorous couples or *mithuna*. There are various interpretations of these erotic sculptures in temple architecture, but it is difficult to limit the theory to one only. (see Introduction, pp. 18-20)

91-92. Amorous couples or *mithuna*. Some postures can be identified with the poses suggested in the *Kāmasūtra*, but not necessarily Śāstric in nature in case of these sculptures.

93. Tāntric *mithuna* figures in a row.

94. Acrobatic posture of *mithuna*.

95. Sunrise at the Koṇārka beach on Candrabhāgā-yātrā day. Pilgrims gather here since the previous night of the seventh day of the bright half of Māgha (*Māgha Śukla Saptamī*) or the day of Candrabhāgā-yātrā to worship the rising sun, the birth of Sūrya.

96. Bathing at the shore. According to *Prācī Mahātmya* of *Padma Purāṇa*, Sāmba is said to have worshipped the Sun on the bank of the sacred Candrabhāgā River and was cured of leprosy. It is believed that bathing at the shore on the Candrabhāgā-yātrā day makes a man free from all sins and diseases.

97. A wishing lamp and incense sticks are lit, in dedication to the Sun-God, Sūrya, who appears from the blue sea riding his chariot drawn by seven horses.

98. Ladies drawing ritualistic figures on the sand to invoke the Sun Deity to the spot. Geometric motifs are common to the ritualistic floor paintings, *cittā* or *jhothi* in Orissa, generally known as *kolam* in the South, and *raṅgolī* in the North.

99. Pilgrims gathering to observe the ancestral rite. This is also the day to worship their ancestors and to propitiate the departed souls.

100. Procession of the pilgrims to the Candrabhāgā near the seashore.

101. Pilgrims gathering around the first frontal wheel of the Temple. Knowledge of history, art and culture, mythology, rites and rituals is firmly transferred in this way through visiting actual sites and seeing the buildings and sculptures.

102. An unusual crowd gathered on the festive day. The religious act of pilgrimage is seen as being combined also with cultural tourism and recreation for the people.

103. An Odissi dancer on the beach poses against the rising sun. Dance postures of Odissi have been obviously taken from the sculptural panels of Naṭa Mandira of Koṇārka and others, as this style of dance has been revived based on these sculptures.

Plates

Photographs: OKI Morihiro

1. Sūrya Temple complex at Koṇārka, an aerial view.

2. (*Next page*)
Roof of the Hall or *mukhaśālā*.

4. Horses in front of the Hall pulling the chariot-temple.

◂
3. (*Previous page*)
Southern side-view of the Temple.

5. Naṭa Mandira or Festive Hall seen from the south-east.

6. Lions pouncing over elephants in front of Naṭa Mandira.

7. Frontal view of Naṭa Mandira seen from the east.

8. Original ceiling of Naṭa Mandira, now in the Koṇārka Site Museum.

9. Naṭa Mandira seen from the west.

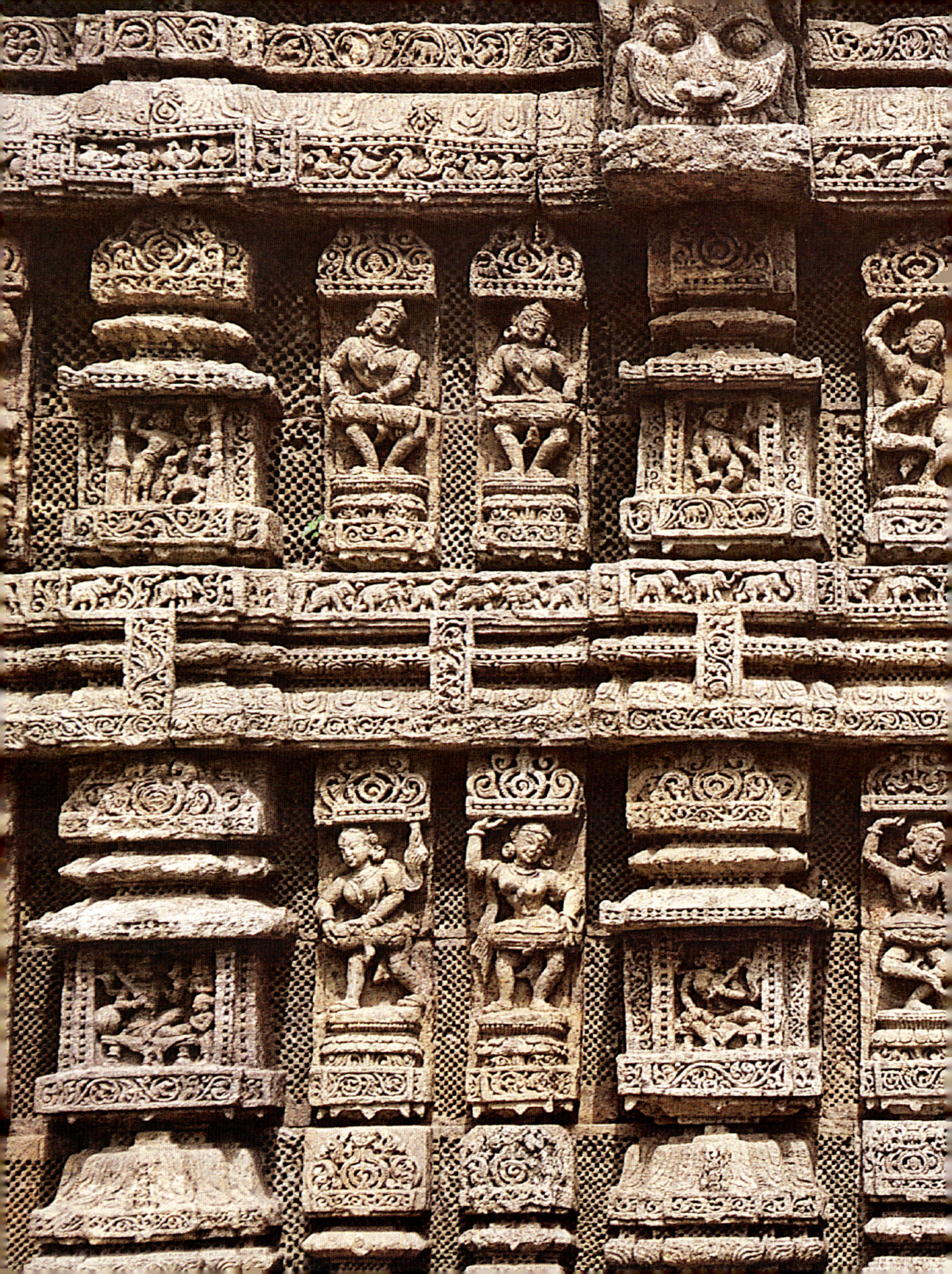

11. Bracket above the upper *bāḍa* or platform of Naṭa Mandira.

12. Śiva in an inset of the basement.

10. (*Previous page*)
Rows of musicians and dancers on the base wall of Naṭa Mandira.

13. (*Next page*)
Kṛṣṇa

14. Musicians.

15. Musicians.

16. A player of *kahalā*.

17. Musician-dancers.

18. Musician-dancers.

19. Musicians.

20. Female musician.

21.
Southern side
of *mukhaśālā*.

22. Southern wall of *mukhaśālā.*

23. First frontal wheel on the Southern wall.

24. Middle of the Southern wall.

25-26. Medallions on the spoke.

27-28. Medallions on the spoke.

29-30. Medallions on the frame.

31. Basement frieze below the wheel.

32-34. Basement friezes below the wheel.

35-38. Basement friezes below the wheel.

39-41. Three photos showing *Navagraha* or the Nine Planets originally set above the central door-jamb. ▸
(now removed: see 42 below)

42. *Navagraha* on the door-jamb photographically restored in original position.

45. (*Next page*)
Sūrya as Mitra on the wall of the Southern Side-Temple.

44. Detail of the left frieze of door-jamb.

43. Friezes of the central door-jamb.

45.
Sūrya as Mitra on the wall of the Southern Side-Temple.

46. Detail of Mitra.

47. Seven horses under the Deity to pull the chariot.

48. Sūrya as Pūṣan on the wall of the Wester Side-Temple.

49. Detail of Pūṣan.

50. Sūrya as Haridaśva on the wall of the Northern Side-Temple.

51. Detail of *siṁhāsana* of the ruined sanctuary.

52. Full view of the *siṁhāsana* or pedestal for the main Deity.

53. A panel on the wall.

54. Apsaras or heavenly musician playing *kahalā* at the *cāla* recess on the roof.

55. A lady drummer (Apsaras or heavenly musician).

56. Upper portions of *mukhaśālā* showing tiered *pīḍha, ghaṇṭīcāla* (bell-shaped roof) and *āmalaka*.

57. Heavenly musicians in the recess of the middle row of *cāla*.

58. (*Next page*)
Bhairava and musicians
in the recess of the *cāla*.

59. Heavenly musician (Apsaras) on the tier.

60. Heavenly musician (Apsaras) on the tier.

61. Heavenly musician (Apsaras) on the tier.

62. Apsaras playing cymbals.

63. Mārtaṇḍa-Bhairava, a side view.

64. Sculptural panels and pilasters on the wall.

65. *Sūtradhāra* or the Architect with his wife.

66. Foreign delegates bringing tributes to the king, including a giraffe.

67. An old lady departing for pilgrimage taking leave of her family.

69. *Kanyā* or a maiden putting earrings.

◂
68. (*Previous page*)
*Alasākanyā*s or the graceful maidens.

70. Joy of life.

71. *Ḍālamālikā* or *kanyā* holding a branch of tree.

72. *Nūpurapādikā* or *kanyā* removing the anklets.

73. *Darpaṇā* or *kanyā* looking into the mirror.

74. A naked woman standing over a flame.

75. Warriors with horse.

76. Galloping horse pulling the chariot-temple.

77. Mighty elephant overpowering an enemy.

79. *Virāla* or composite mythical animal trampling on a demon or evil-doer (*dharmavirāla*).

◂
78. Lion pouncing over an elephant.

80. Giraffe or winged antelope — a rare motif.

81. *Nāga* and *Nāginī*, or serpent couples.

82. Amorous couples with *Nāga -Nāginī*.

83. Amorous *Nāga-Nāginī* couple and a musician.

84. Amorous *Nāga-Nāginī*.

85. Amorous *Nāga-Nāginī*.

86. Amorous couples or *mithuna*.

87. Amorous couple or *mithuna*.

88. Amorous couple or *mithuna*.

89. Amorous couple or *mithuna*.

90. Amorous couple or *mithuna*.

91. Amorous couple or *mithuna*.

92. Amorous couple or *mithuna*.

93. Tantric *mithuna* figures in row.

94. Acrobatic posture of a *mithuna* couple.

95. Sunrise at the Koṇārka Beach on *Chandrabhāgā-yātrā* day.

96. Bathing at the shore.

97. A wishing lamp and incense lit on the occasion.

98. Drawing ritualistic figures on the sand.

▸
99. (*Next page*)
Pilgrims gathering to observe
the ancestral rite.

100. Pilgrims' procession to the seashore.

101. Pilgrims gathering around the first wheel.

102. Unusual crowd on the festive day.

103. Odissi dancer against the rising sun.

Glossary

ācārya : teacher.

adbhuta : the sentiment of wonder or surprise.

Āditya : the name of the Sun-God in the Veda.

ādivāsī : original inhabitants of the land.

alasākanyā : "graceful maiden," term used in the Orissan Śilpaśāstras for the female figures, in other parts (Western Indian texts) called *surasundarī* (divine beauties).

āmalaka : myrobalan fruit; circular crowning part of the temple in the shape of a fluted disk with sections, resembling the *āmalaka* fruit.

ānanda : bliss, joy.

Apsaras : heavenly musicians and dancers, female counterpart of Gandharvas (Vedic).

arka : the sun.

bāḍa : wall.

Bhairava : a terrific and protective form of Śiva.

Bhāskara : lit. "maker of the light," name of the Sun-God.

bhāva : emotion.

cakrapīṭha : elevated platform on which the temple stands, technical term for the platform of the Koṇārka temple.

Candrabhāgā-yātrā : pilgrimage to the sacred river Candrabhāgā running by the side of Koṇārka (now dried up).

cāla : roof with horizontal tiers.

cidarka : the Sun of consciousness.

ḍālamālikā : *kanyā* (maiden) holding a branch of a tree.

darpaṇa : mirror.

darpaṇā : *kanyā* looking into a mirror.

deul (Oriya) : temple (Skt. *devālaya*, "abode of the gods").

devadāsī : female temple servant, temple dancers.

dharmavirāla : a composite figure trampling on a human body representing evil (*pāpapuruṣa*).

dhyāna : Meditation; a verse describing a divine image, hense *dhyāna-śloka*.

dikpāla : guardian of the eight directions.

gaja-siṁha : lion on the back of an elephant.

garbhagṛha : "womb-chamber"; sanctum of the temple containing the main image or *liṅga*.

gavākṣa : window, structural opening in the temple wall.

ghaṇṭicāla : bell-shaped roof.

ghaṭa : earthen pot, used also as a percussion instrument.

grāmadevatā : village deities.

hāsya : the sentiment of humour.

jagamohana (Oriya): colloquial term for *mukhaśālā*, front hall.

jāṅgha : "shin;" the vertical wall-part of the temple (above the base and below the curvilinear spire).

kahalā : a wind-instrument similar to the present *śahanāī*.

kalaśa : vase, pot; crowning part of the temple, symbolizing the vase of fullness.

kāmabandha : love images, erotic couples.

kāmakalā : "the art of love"; a tāntric tradition involving sexual ritual.

kanyā : maiden, female figure.

karaṇa : dance poses.

karuṇa rasa : the sentiment of sorrow and compassion.

koṇa : corner.

kṣetra : sacred field, holy place of pilgrimage.

kula/kaula : Tantric traditions.

kuṇḍalinī : divine energy (*śakti*) residing in the human body, which can be raised by *yoga*.

Māgha : Hindu month falling in January-February.

mantra : sacred word, ritual formula.

mithuna : erotic couple.

mṛdaṅga : horizontal drum.

mukhaśālā : 'main hall,' the front part of the temple, hall for the devotees.

mūlasūtra : fundamental unit of measurement (for the construction of the temple)

mūrti : divine image.

nāda : sound.

nāga/nāginī : mythical serpents with human head, profusely depicted on Orissan temples.

Nāgara : North Indian temple style.

Naṭa Mandira : Dance Temple, hall in front of the temple for music and dance as part of the worship.

Navagraha : the nine planets.

nūpurapādikā : *kanyā* (maiden) putting on anklets.

pābhāga : 'foot-part,' base of the temple (see *pañcakarma*).

pañcakarma : five mouldings of the base of the temple, symbolizing the five elements.

pañcaratha : temple design with five vertical projections on the *śikhara* or *vimāna*.

pārśva-devatā : secondary images representing aspects of the main deity.

pīḍha : flat tiers as components of the roof of the Mukhaśālā.

prāsāda : palace; temple.

pūjā : ritual worship.

purohita : priest.

rasa : aesthetic emotion; the *Nāṭyaśāstra* lists eight or nine fundamental *rasa*s.

rekha : "line"; style of the North-Indian spire (*śikhara*) with vertical divisions creating lines.

ṛṣi : sage, seer, poets of the Veda.

ṛta : cosmic order.

sādhanā : spiritual practice.

śakti : divine energy; consort of a male god.

sandhisthāna : the juncture between the two major parts of the temple (Mukhaśālā and *vimāna*).

sandhyā : twilight, auspicious time for worship; one of the consorts of Sūrya.

śānta : the peaceful sentiment.

Savitṛ : Vedic form of Sūrya, lit. the impeller.

siddhi : perfection, spiritual accomplishment, yogic powers.

śikhara : spire, the tall spire above the sanctum (also *vimāna*).

śilpin / śilpī : artist, sculptor.

siṁhāsana : throne or pedestal (because it is often supported by legs in the form of lion's paws).

sthāpaka : architect.

sthapati : architect and sculptor.

sūtradhāra : lit. "holder of the thread"; chief architect; in the context of theatre, the stage-director.

tāla : rhythmic cycle for keeping time with music and dance.

tithi : lunar day.

tribhaṅga : body pose with three bends.

Uṣas : the Goddess of Dawn (*Ṛgveda*); one of the Śaktis of Sūrya.

vāhana : animal vehicle of the deity.

vimāna : lit. vehicle; temple spire above the sanctum or *garbhagṛha*.

vīṇā : string instrument of ancient origin.

vīra : the heroic sentiment.

virāla : mythical composite animal figure, or human-animal combined, having an apotropaic function at the temple (mostly at the base and in the recesses).

yakṣiṇī : feminine spirit represented in early Indian art, along with *yakṣa* (masculine form).

yantra : ritual diagram.

Bibliography

Acharya, P.K. (1927-1933), *Indian Architecture — Mānasāra*, et al., 5 vols. New Delhi: Oxford University Press.

Anand, Mulk Raj (1958), *Kama Kala*, Geneva: Nagel Publishers.

Banerjea, J.N. (1956), *The Development of Hindu Iconography*, Calcutta: Calcutta University.

———, (1984), "Sūrya, Ādityas and the Navagrahas," *Journal of Indian Society of Oriental Art*, vol. XVII.

Behera, Karuna Sagar (1992), *Temples of Orissa*, Bhubaneswar.

———, K.S. (1996), *The Heritage of Mankind: Konarak*, 2 vols. New Delhi: Aryan Books International.

Behera, K.S. & Thomas Donaldson (1998), *Sculpture Masterpieces from Orissa: Style and Iconography*, New Delhi: Aryan Books International.

Boner, Alice and Sadaśiva Rath Sarma with Rajendra Prasad Das (1972), *New Light on the Sun Temple of Koṇārka*, Varanasi: Chowkhamba Sanskrit Series Office.

Boner, Alice and Sadasiva Rath Sarma, ed. by Bettina Bäumer, Rajendra Prasada Das and Sadananda Das (2004, second revised edn.), *Śilpa Prakāśa, Medieval Orissan Sanskrit Text on Temple Architecture by Rāmacandra Mahāpātra Kaula Bhaṭṭāraka*, New Delhi: IGNCA and Motilal Banarsidass (first edn. 1966, Leiden: Brill).

Bose, Nirmal Kumar (1932), *Canons of Orissan Architecture*, Calcutta: R. Chatterjee (rept., 1982, New Delhi: Cosmo Publications).

Brown, Percy (1959), *Indian Architecture: Buddhist and Hindu Periods*. Bombay: Taraporewalla & Sons.

Coomaraswamy, Ananda Kumar (1927), *History of Indian and Indonesian Art*. London: Edward Goldson (reprint 1965, New York: Dover Publications).

———, (1992), *Essays in Early Indian Architecture*, ed. by M.W. Meister, New Delhi: IGNCA.

———, (1995), *Ananda Coomaraswamy: Essays in Architectural Theory*, ed. M.W. Meister, Delhi: Oxford University Press.

Dehejia, Vidya (1979), *Early Stone Temples in Orissa*, New Delhi: Vikas Publications.

Desai, Devangana (1975), *Erotic Sculpture of India: A Social-Cultural Study*, New Delhi: Munshiram Manoharlal.

Donaldson, Thomas (1985-1987), *Hindu Temple Art of Orissa*, 3 vols. Leiden: Brill.

———, (1988), "Ganga Monarch and a Monumental Sun Temple," *Marg: Royal Patrons and Great Temple Art*, ed. by Vidya Dehejia, Bombay: Marg Publications, pp. 125-43.

———, (2002), *Tantra and Śākta Art of Orissa*, New Delhi: D.K. Printworld.

———, (2003), *Monumental Legacy: Konark*, New Delhi: Oxford University Press.

Elisofon, Eliot and Alan Watts (1971), *The Temple of Konarak: Erotic Spirituality*. New Delhi: Vikas Publications.

Fergusson, James (1910), *A History of Indian and Eastern Architecture*, London: John Murray (rept., 1967, Delhi: Munshiram Manoharlal).

Gangoly, Ordhendra C. (1956), *Koṇārak*, Calcutta: Jiten Bose.

Ganguly, Manmohan (1912), *Orissa and her Remains*, Calcutta/London: Thacker Spink & Co.

Gopinath Rao, T.A., (1914-15), *Elements of Hindu Iconography*, 2 vols. 4 parts, Madras (rept., 1968, New York: Paragon; etc.).

Gupta, Shakti M. (1977), *Surya: The Sun God,* Bombay: Somaiya Publications.

Ingalls, Daniel H., Jeffery Masson & M.V. Pathwardhan, tran. (1990), *The Dhvanyāloka of Ānandavardhana with Locana of Abhinavagupta.* Cambridge: Harvard University Press.

Kramrisch, Stella (1946), *The Hindu Temple,* 2 vols. Calcutta: University of Calcutta.

Lal, Kanwar (1967), *Miracle of Konarak,* Delhi: Asia Press.

Mahāpātra, Sthāpaka Nirañjana (1994), *Śilparatnakośa, A Glossary of Orissan Temple Architecture,* ed. and tran. by Bettina Bäumer and Rajendra Prasad Das, New Delhi: IGNCA and Motilal Banarsidass.

Marg (1968), *Koṇārak,* ed. by Vidya Dehejia, Bombay: Marg Publications.

Mehta, Rustam J. (1969), *Konarak: The Sun Temple of Love,* Bombay: D.B. Taraporewalla & Sons.

Meister, M.W., M.A. Dhaky & Krishna Deva (1981), *Encychopaedia of Indian Architecture,* 2 vols. 6 parts, New Delhi: American Institute of Indian Studies.

Mitra, Debala (1976), *Konarak,* New Delhi: Archaeological Survey of India, second edn.

Mitra, Rajendralala (1875), *The Antiquities of Orissa,* 2 vols. Calcutta (rpt., 1961-2, Calcutta: Indian Studies Past and Present, Firma KLM).

Mohapatra, Ramesh Prasad (1989), *Temple Legends of Orissa,* Bhubaneswar: Orissa Sahitya Akademi.

Pandey, D.P. (1939), *Iconographical Study of the Indian Sun-God,* Leiden: Brill.

Panikkar, Raimundo (1977), *The Vedic Experience,* London: DLT (several rpts., Delhi: Motilal Banarsidass; et al.).

Rowland, Benjamin (1970), *The Art and Architecture of India,* London: Penguin Books.

Sarangi, S.N. (1990), *Konark Masterplan and Tourist Guide on Golden Triangle; Konark-Puri-Bhubaneswar,* Bhubaneswar: Author.

Sarasvati, S.K. (1957), *Survey of Indian Sculpture,* Calcutta: Calcutta University.

Sivaramamurti, C. (1961), *Indian Sculpture,* New Delhi: Allied Publishers.

Soundara Rajan, K.V. (1984), *Early Kalinga Art and Architecture*, Delhi: Sundeep Prakashan.

Srivastava, V.C. (1972), *Sun Worship in Ancient India*, Allahabad: Indological Publications.

Swarup, B. (1910), *Konarak: The Black Pagoda*, Cuttack.

Thomas, Lowell (1930), *India, Land of the Black Pagoda*, New York.

Vatsyayan, Kapila (1968), *Classical Indian Dance in Literature and the Arts*. New Delhi: Sangeet Natak Akademi.

Zimmer, Heinrich (1946), *Myth and Symbols in Indian Art and Civilization*. Washington DC: Bollingen Foundation (rpt. 1962, New York: Harper).

———, (1955), *Art of Indian Asia*, 2 vols. Washington DC: Bollingen Foundation; New York: Pantheon Books.